Learning to Read, Step by Step!

Ready to Read   Preschool–Kindergarten
• big type and easy words • rhyme and rhythm • picture clues
For children who know the alphabet and are eager to begin reading.

Reading with Help   Preschool–Grade 1
• basic vocabulary • short sentences • simple stories
For children who recognize familiar words and sound out new words with help.

Reading on Your Own   Grades 1–3
• engaging characters • easy-to-follow plots • popular topics
For children who are ready to read on their own.

Reading Paragraphs   Grades 2–3
• challenging vocabulary • short paragraphs • exciting stories
For newly independent readers who read simple sentences with confidence.

Ready for Chapters   Grades 2–4
• chapters • longer paragraphs • full-color art
For children who want to take the plunge into chapter books but still like colorful pictures.

STEP INTO READING® is designed to give every child a successful reading experience. The grade levels are only guides; children will progress through the steps at their own speed, developing confidence in their reading. The F&P Text Level on the back cover serves as another tool to help you choose the right book for your child.

Remember, a lifetime love of reading starts with a single step!

For writers of all ages and all creeds. Remember the moments in your life that are like a rainbow, moments that "defy the skill of pen or pencil"— and write about them anyway, just as Frederick Douglass did.
—F.M.

Dedicated to the spirit of Frederick's love for his mother, and the love of reading I hope will grow in the hearts of all who read this book.
—N.T.

Acknowledgments: With gratitude to my friend Amy Smith, for guiding me toward this story. To my family and my many friends in teaching and writing, for their readings and support. To my editors, Anna Membrino and Heidi Kilgras, for their expert collaboration and always believing in me. And to Andrew Sargent, Associate Professor at West Chester University, Pennsylvania, for his expertise. Three books were most valuable to me: *My Bondage and My Freedom* and *Narrative of the Life of Frederick Douglass*, both by Frederick Douglass, and *Frederick Douglass: Prophet of Freedom* by David W. Blight.

Visit us on the Web!
StepIntoReading.com
rhcbooks.com

Educators and librarians, for a variety of teaching tools, visit us at RHTeachersLibrarians.com

Library of Congress Cataloging-in-Publication Data
Names: Murphy, Frank, author. | Tadgell, Nicole, illustrator.
Title: Frederick Douglass: voice for justice, voice for freedom / by Frank Murphy; illustrations by Nicole Tadgell.
Description: New York: Random House, [2019] | Series: Step into reading. Step 3 |
Audience: Ages: 5 to 8.
Identifiers: LCCN 2019008067 (print) | LCCN 2019012899 (ebook) | ISBN 978-1-5247-7235-2 (pbk.) | ISBN 978-1-5247-7236-9 (library binding) | ISBN 978-1-5247-7237-6 (ebook)
Subjects: LCSH: Douglass, Frederick, 1818–1895—Juvenile literature. | African American abolitionists—Biography—Juvenile literature. | Abolitionists—United States—Biography—Juvenile literature. | Antislavery movements—United States—Juvenile literature.
Classification: LCC E449.D75 (ebook) | LCC E449.D75 M87 2019 (print) | DDC 973.8092 [B]—dc23

Printed in the United States of America

10 9 8 7 6 5 4 3 2 1

This book has been officially leveled by using the F&P Text Level Gradient™ Leveling System.

Frederick Douglass

Voice for Justice, Voice for Freedom

by Frank Murphy
illustrated by Nicole Tadgell

Random House New York

This is the story of how
Frederick Douglass,
who was once
an enslaved person,
helped outlaw slavery
in America.

In the early 1600s,
some White people
bought kidnapped people
from many African countries
and brought them to America.

It was cruel.
These White people
sold the Africans
to other people
to work for them.
They treated them
as property
and did not pay them
for their work.
This is called "slavery."

Frederick Douglass's mother,

Harriet Bailey,

was born into slavery.

That meant Frederick

was born into slavery, too.

The people who
owned Frederick
did not tell him
his exact birthday.
Frederick thought
he was born sometime
in 1817.

Many slaveholders did not
care enough
to keep enslaved families together.
Frederick did not
live with his mother.
He only got to see her
a few times in his life.

One day,
Frederick was being
unfairly punished
by a woman
who was enslaved, too.
He was not allowed to eat.

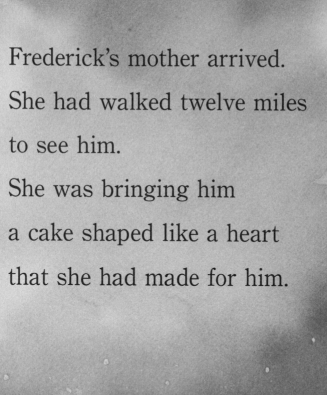

Frederick's mother arrived.
She had walked twelve miles
to see him.
She was bringing him
a cake shaped like a heart
that she had made for him.

When she saw
what this woman
was doing to her son,
she was very angry.

She told the woman
never to punish him
like that again.

Enslaved people
were not supposed
to learn to read and write.
But the wife
of Frederick's slaveholder
taught Frederick the alphabet.
She began teaching him
to read.

She stopped
their lessons as soon as
her husband found out.

He and some
other slaveholders
were afraid that
if Black people did learn,
they would have the tools
to resist being enslaved.

But Frederick found
other ways to learn.
He gave bread to
poor White children he met
when he went on errands.
They gave Frederick
reading lessons in return.

At a shipyard,
Frederick watched
shipbuilders writing
letters on wood.
Then he used chalk
to copy what they wrote.

By the time
Frederick was sixteen,
he had grown strong
and tall.
His mind had
grown strong, too.

Frederick's slaveholder
was worried that he was
learning too much.
So he sent Frederick
to work for a different man.

The man was paid
to teach Frederick a lesson:
that he was a slave
and nothing more.
This man beat Frederick
many times.

One day,
Frederick made a brave
but risky choice.
When the man beat him,
Frederick fought back—
and won.
After that,
this slaveholder never
laid a hand on him again.

Frederick kept reading.
The more he read,
the more he learned.
He knew that White people
were not better than Black people.
He knew that all people
should be treated equally.
And he knew that people
should not be enslaved.

Years later,
Frederick was able
to escape north,
to a state
where slavery was
against the law.

He had met a free woman
named Anna Murray.
She was a housekeeper.
She helped him escape.

She snuck a sailor's uniform

from her laundry pile

so Frederick could wear it

as a disguise.

The disguise

and some documents

allowed him to escape!

Twelve days later,

Frederick married Anna.

In New York,

Frederick met people

who wanted to abolish slavery.

These people were called

"abolitionists."

"Abolish" means "end."

Frederick told the abolitionists
his story.

The abolitionists
asked Frederick
to give speeches
about his life.
He was a powerful speaker.

They knew he could
help others realize
that slavery was wrong.
Soon, Frederick was
giving speeches to thousands
of people.

Frederick wrote a book.
It described
what he went through
as an enslaved person
and his triumphs
in his fight for freedom.
It is called
*Narrative of the Life
of Frederick Douglass,
an American Slave.*

People all over the country
and across the world
read it.
Because of Frederick's book
and the speeches he gave,
more people began
to understand that
slavery was wrong.

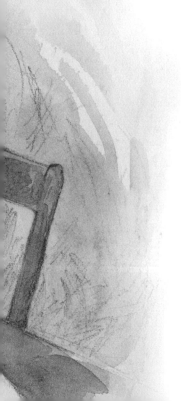

Frederick and Anna
had five children.
Anna and the children
helped Frederick
fight against slavery.
Their home in
Rochester, New York,
was a "station" on the
Underground Railroad.

This was not
an actual railroad.
It is the name
of a network
of people
and safe houses
on the route north
to freedom.
These brave people
helped the enslaved escape.

Four of Frederick's children
helped him publish
an anti-slavery newspaper.
It was called the *North Star*.

Lewis and Frederick Jr. helped print
the newspapers.
Rosetta folded them.
Charles delivered them.

The Civil War started in 1861.

Most people from the North were
fighting to end slavery.

Most people from the South were
fighting to keep it.

Frederick wrote articles
and gave speeches
inspiring Black men
to become soldiers.
He even met with
President Abraham Lincoln
to convince him that
Black soldiers
should be treated
the same as White soldiers.

Soon, many more Black men
were fighting for the North.
Over the next four years,
200,000 Black soldiers
helped the North win the war
and preserve the United States.

Two of those soldiers were

Frederick's sons

Charles and Lewis!

After the enslaved people were freed,

Frederick argued that

Black men should be

given the right to vote.

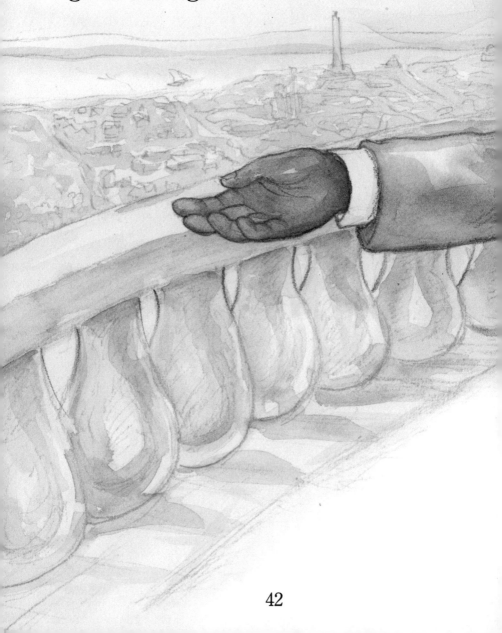

He helped convince
President
Ulysses S. Grant.
Congress amended
the Constitution
to make it a law.

Frederick made history

in lots of ways.

But not many people

know about this:

When Frederick was

a grown man,

he decided to choose

a birthday for himself.

Frederick thought about
his mother.
He remembered that day
she came to his rescue.
It was in February.
He remembered the
heart-shaped cake
she had made for him.

Frederick decided to
honor that memory
of his mother
and the love she showed him.
He chose February 14
as his "official" birthday—
Valentine's Day.

AUTHOR'S NOTE

For most of his life, Frederick believed he was born in 1817. A document written by Frederick's slaveholder was discovered later, saying Frederick's birth was in February 1818. Most historians believe this document proves that Frederick was born in 1818.

In 1926, Black History Week was created. A historian named Carter G. Woodson was part of the group that established it. Woodson chose the week that included President Lincoln's birthday, February 12, and the birthday Frederick chose, February 14. Years later, February became Black History Month—a month to celebrate the important contributions of Black Americans.